Academic Planner

for University
and Career Minded Students

Activinotes

Activinotes

DAILY JOURNALS, PLANNERS, NOTEBOOKS AND OTHER BLANK BOOKS

Copyright 2016

Notes

Jots

Reminders

To do List

To do list :

Date/Time	Subject	Activity	Notes

Notes :

_____
_____
_____
_____
_____
_____
_____

Quiz and Exam Schedulles :

Assignments :

Subjects to Review :

Jots & Notes

To do list :

Date/Time	Subject	Activity	Notes

Notes :

_____
_____
_____
_____
_____
_____
_____

Quiz and Exam Schedulles :

Assignments :

Subjects to Review :

Jots & Notes

To do list :

Date/Time	Subject	Activity	Notes

Notes :

_____
_____
_____
_____
_____
_____
_____

Quiz and Exam Schedulles :

Assignments :

Subjects to Review :

Jots & Notes

To do list :

Date/Time	Subject	Activity	Notes

Notes :

_____
_____
_____
_____
_____
_____
_____

Quiz and Exam Schedulles :

Assignments :

Subjects to Review :

Jots & Notes

To do list :

Date/Time	Subject	Activity	Notes

Notes :

_____
_____
_____
_____
_____
_____
_____

Quiz and Exam Schedulles :

Assignments :

Subjects to Review :

Jots & Notes

To do list :

Date/Time	Subject	Activity	Notes

Notes :

_____
_____
_____
_____
_____
_____
_____

Quiz and Exam Schedulles :

Assignments :

Subjects to Review :

Jots & Notes

To do list :

Date/Time	Subject	Activity	Notes

Notes :

_____
_____
_____
_____
_____
_____
_____

Quiz and Exam Schedulles :

Assignments :

Subjects to Review :

Jots & Notes

To do list :

Date/Time	Subject	Activity	Notes

Notes :

_____
_____
_____
_____
_____
_____
_____

Quiz and Exam Schedulles :

Assignments :

Subjects to Review :

Jots & Notes

To do list :

Date/Time	Subject	Activity	Notes

Notes :

_____
_____
_____
_____
_____
_____
_____

Quiz and Exam Schedulles :

Assignments :

Subjects to Review :

Jots & Notes

To do list :

Date/Time	Subject	Activity	Notes

Notes :

Quiz and Exam Schedulles :

Assignments :

Subjects to Review :

Jots & Notes

To do list :

Date/Time	Subject	Activity	Notes

Notes :

_____
_____
_____
_____
_____
_____
_____

Quiz and Exam Schedulles :

Assignments :

Subjects to Review :

Jots & Notes

To do list :

Date/Time	Subject	Activity	Notes

Notes :

_____
_____
_____
_____
_____
_____
_____

Quiz and Exam Schedulles :

Assignments :

Subjects to Review :

Jots & Notes

To do list :

Date/Time	Subject	Activity	Notes

Notes :

_____
_____
_____
_____
_____
_____
_____

Quiz and Exam Schedulles :

Assignments :

Subjects to Review :

Jots & Notes

Date/Time	Subject	Activity	Notes

Notes :

_____
_____
_____
_____
_____
_____
_____

Quiz and Exam Schedulles :

Assignments :

Subjects to Review :

Jots & Notes

To do list :

Date/Time	Subject	Activity	Notes

Notes :

Quiz and Exam Schedulles :

Assignments :

Subjects to Review :

Jots & Notes

To do list :

Date/Time	Subject	Activity	Notes

Notes :

_____
_____
_____
_____
_____
_____
_____

Quiz and Exam Schedulles :

Assignments :

Subjects to Review :

Jots & Notes

To do list :

Date/Time	Subject	Activity	Notes

Notes :

_____
_____
_____
_____
_____
_____
_____

Quiz and Exam Schedulles :

Assignments :

Subjects to Review :

Jots & Notes

To do list :

Date/Time	Subject	Activity	Notes

Notes :

_____
_____
_____
_____
_____
_____
_____

Quiz and Exam Schedulles :

Assignments :

Subjects to Review :

Jots & Notes

To do list :

Date/Time	Subject	Activity	Notes

Notes :

Quiz and Exam Schedulles :

Assignments :

Subjects to Review :

Jots & Notes

To do list :

Date/Time	Subject	Activity	Notes

Notes :

_____
_____
_____
_____
_____
_____
_____

Quiz and Exam Schedulles :

Assignments :

Subjects to Review :

Jots & Notes

To do list :

Date/Time	Subject	Activity	Notes

Notes :

_____
_____
_____
_____
_____
_____
_____

Quiz and Exam Schedulles :

Assignments :

Subjects to Review :

Jots & Notes

To do list :

Date/Time	Subject	Activity	Notes

Notes :

_____
_____
_____
_____
_____
_____
_____

Quiz and Exam Schedulles :

Assignments :

Subjects to Review :

Jots & Notes

To do list :

Date/Time	Subject	Activity	Notes

Notes :

_____
_____
_____
_____
_____
_____
_____

Quiz and Exam Schedulles :

Assignments :

Subjects to Review :

Jots & Notes

To do list :

Date/Time	Subject	Activity	Notes

Notes :

_____
_____
_____
_____
_____
_____
_____

Quiz and Exam Schedulles :

Assignments :

Subjects to Review :

Jots & Notes

To do list :

Date/Time	Subject	Activity	Notes

Notes :

_____
_____
_____
_____
_____
_____
_____

Quiz and Exam Schedulles :

Assignments :

Subjects to Review :

Jots & Notes

To do list :

Date/Time	Subject	Activity	Notes

Notes :

Quiz and Exam Schedulles :

Assignments :

Subjects to Review :

Jots & Notes

Date/Time	Subject	Activity	Notes

Notes :

_____
_____
_____
_____
_____
_____
_____

Quiz and Exam Schedulles :

Assignments :

Subjects to Review :

Jots & Notes

Date/Time	Subject	Activity	Notes

Notes :

_____
_____
_____
_____
_____
_____
_____

Quiz and Exam Schedulles :

Assignments :

Subjects to Review :

Jots & Notes

To do list :

Date/Time	Subject	Activity	Notes

Notes :

_____
_____
_____
_____
_____
_____
_____

Quiz and Exam Schedulles :

Assignments :

Subjects to Review :

Jots & Notes

To do list :

Date/Time	Subject	Activity	Notes

Notes :

_____
_____
_____
_____
_____
_____
_____

Quiz and Exam Schedulles :

Assignments :

Subjects to Review :

Jots & Notes

Date/Time	Subject	Activity	Notes

Notes :

_____
_____
_____
_____
_____
_____
_____

Quiz and Exam Schedulles :

Assignments :

Subjects to Review :

Jots & Notes

To do list :

Date/Time	Subject	Activity	Notes

Notes :

_____
_____
_____
_____
_____
_____
_____

Quiz and Exam Schedulles :

Assignments :

Subjects to Review :

Jots & Notes

To do list :

Date/Time	Subject	Activity	Notes

Notes :

_____
_____
_____
_____
_____
_____
_____

Quiz and Exam Schedulles :

Assignments :

Subjects to Review :

Jots & Notes

To do list :

Date/Time	Subject	Activity	Notes

Notes :

_____
_____
_____
_____
_____
_____
_____

Quiz and Exam Schedulles :

Assignments :

Subjects to Review :

Jots & Notes

To do list :

Date/Time	Subject	Activity	Notes

Notes :

_____
_____
_____
_____
_____
_____
_____

Quiz and Exam Schedulles :

Assignments :

Subjects to Review :

Jots & Notes

To do list :

Date/Time	Subject	Activity	Notes

Notes :

_____
_____
_____
_____
_____
_____
_____

Quiz and Exam Schedulles :

Assignments :

Subjects to Review :

Jots & Notes

To do list :

Date/Time	Subject	Activity	Notes

Notes :

_____
_____
_____
_____
_____
_____
_____

Quiz and Exam Schedulles :

Assignments :

Subjects to Review :

Jots & Notes

To do list :

Date/Time	Subject	Activity	Notes

Notes :

_____
_____
_____
_____
_____
_____
_____

Quiz and Exam Schedulles :

Assignments :

Subjects to Review :

Jots & Notes

Date/Time	Subject	Activity	Notes

Notes :

_____

_____

_____

_____

_____

_____

_____

Quiz and Exam Schedulles :

Assignments :

Subjects to Review :

Jots & Notes

To do list :

Date/Time	Subject	Activity	Notes

Notes :

_____
_____
_____
_____
_____
_____
_____

Quiz and Exam Schedulles :

Assignments :

Subjects to Review :

Jots & Notes

To do list :

Date/Time	Subject	Activity	Notes

Notes :

_____
_____
_____
_____
_____
_____
_____

Quiz and Exam Schedulles :

Assignments :

Subjects to Review :

Jots & Notes

To do list :

Date/Time	Subject	Activity	Notes

Notes :

_____

_____

_____

_____

_____

_____

_____

Quiz and Exam Schedulles :

Assignments :

Subjects to Review :

Jots & Notes

To do list :

Date/Time	Subject	Activity	Notes

Notes :

_____
_____
_____
_____
_____
_____
_____

Quiz and Exam Schedulles :

Assignments :

Subjects to Review :

Jots & Notes

Date/Time	Subject	Activity	Notes

Notes :

_____
_____
_____
_____
_____
_____
_____

Quiz and Exam Schedulles :

Assignments :

Subjects to Review :

Jots & Notes

To do list :

Date/Time	Subject	Activity	Notes

Notes :

_____
_____
_____
_____
_____
_____
_____

Quiz and Exam Schedulles :

Assignments :

Subjects to Review :

Jots & Notes

To do list :

Date/Time	Subject	Activity	Notes

Notes :

Quiz and Exam Schedulles :

Assignments :

Subjects to Review :

Jots & Notes

To do list :

Date/Time	Subject	Activity	Notes

Notes :

_____
_____
_____
_____
_____
_____
_____

Quiz and Exam Schedulles :

Assignments :

Subjects to Review :

Jots & Notes

To do list :

Date/Time	Subject	Activity	Notes

Notes :

_____
_____
_____
_____
_____
_____
_____

Quiz and Exam Schedulles :

Assignments :

Subjects to Review :

Jots & Notes

Date/Time	Subject	Activity	Notes

Notes :

_____
_____
_____
_____
_____
_____
_____

Quiz and Exam Schedulles :

Assignments :

Subjects to Review :

Jots & Notes

To do list :

Date/Time	Subject	Activity	Notes

Notes :

_____
_____
_____
_____
_____
_____
_____

Quiz and Exam Schedulles :

Assignments :

Subjects to Review :

Jots & Notes

To do list :

Date/Time	Subject	Activity	Notes

Notes :

_____
_____
_____
_____
_____
_____
_____

Quiz and Exam Schedulles :

Assignments :

Subjects to Review :

Jots & Notes

www.ingramcontent.com/pod-product-compliance
Lightning Source LLC
Chambersburg PA
CBHW081333090426
42737CB00017B/3123